Just Get Me Broke

exercises in haiku.

Asa Morris

ISBN-10: 1729636845

ISBN-13: 978-1729636848

For the world as it was.

ARGUMENT

At some point in 2016, as I watched a finishing machine for nine hours a day, five or six days a week, I began to write haiku. The counting calmed me. Made me less anxious, focused my thoughts. This is a collection of my first attempts, written over the course of a year or so. They could be worse. Hopefully, anyway.

-A.
06.16.2017

I initially left this collection unpublished. A proof copy sat on my bookshelf for a number of years. The subject matter was a point of shame for me for a long time, and I had to rectify and reconcile a great deal before I was finally able to look at these and see them for what I intended them to be: fledgling attempts at observation through a fog.

      I hope you enjoy them, or at the least, appreciate them for what they are.

-A.
03.27.21

At the Bar.

Crowd repeating scenes

fucking millenia old.

Booze and lies and hope.

"Could you believe it?

Could you *even* believe it?"

"No," he said. I watch.

Kill time in the bar.

Have the girl buy me a drink.

I am a real prize.

A drunk I once knew.

He wasn't always this way.

My ex beat his ass.

Four in the morning.

You are on the couch waiting.

I know I am trash.

Drink and run my mouth.

Another morning after.

Just who I am now.

Love

I love you more now

with each day that slips by us.

You are wonderful.

A girl I knew once,

she said I was wonderful.

Not enough, I guess.

Think so much of you

but I'll just get in the way

like I always do.

I used to think love

was all that mattered to me

but no, it's just nice.

Girl sick at the house,

asleep dreaming of lions.

Am I a lion?

Honey eyes, black hair.

Small and full, beautiful girl.

Keep looking at me.

Your hand on my back.

I get ahead of myself.

Can't just let things be.

Tell them I love them.

My friends all know how I feel.

I know I am loved.

Went to New Hampshire

alone to meet an old friend.

Coming home was hard.

The mountains fade out,

the clash on the radio,

the band at the beach.

This is what I want,

how I want life forever.

Nothing more perfect.

I could starve to death,

it would be okay with me

if I died like this.

Sing my fucking songs

drive and drive and drive and drive

into the sunset.

This is love, I think.

What it's like to be happy.

This is who I am.

(but)

Who the fuck am I?

And why do I deserve this?

These things just happen.

Beauty is beauty

when it comes as a surprise.

I won't trust a plan.

Wake in the morning

and I still need to touch you.

You are beautiful.

I sometimes wonder

if you are being modest.

How couldn't you know?

From a Notebook Hidden at Work

Remember thinking

Money wasn't important

and believing it.

Good things and bad things.

Weather and noise and go home.

All in a day's work.

You all got haircuts.

I'll just let mine fall right out.

Let my gut get fat.

Peeled skin looks like scales,

I noticed on my lunch break.

Blown. Late clocking in.

Music louder please.

I can still hear you talking.

I cut myself out.

A perfect day out.

I caught it for a second.

Gone when I get out.

Daydream of dying.

Make a little time go by.

"Oh, I guess he died."

Is it six O'clock?

Goddamn I want to be home.

Asleep, next to you.

The hum of machines.

All voices lost in the noise.

Who cares, anyway?

I'm sure I could work.

Do I mean myself? Or jobs?

Don't know. I. Don't. Know.

In two hours, lunch.

In three hours I'll be back.

In six hours, home.

It's cool. No one knows.

Smile, nod, and go to work.

A normal person.

This place crushes me.

Turns my brain into dust.

Nothing flows from me.

Watch the machine run.

Bark out its language of noise.

I belong to it.

Open bay doors. Air.

Sunlight. Green. Beautiful world.

And I am in here.

Machine runs, sort of.

Sometimes I feel a kinship.

Mostly it tests me.

And we continue

lucky if it just bored me.

It bores into me.

Sun, on the grass, out

only a few feet away.

Maybe tomorrow.

Everyday I stay.

How I know I'm an adult.

Got those bills to pay.

Always watching clocks.

Perpetually waiting

for the next rough day.

A superior

or the mask of it.

It's all in the eyes.

If I had a week

I think I would feel all right.

A week in the sun.

Leave my haiku here

so I must keep coming back.

I could take them home.

Five pages left now

I think I'm done when this is.

A countdown in verse.

Oh, hey, look at you.

Flipping through my shit haiku.

Well, what do I care?

Arts and crafts at work

just keeping my brain awake.

Damned monotony.

Do you think that if

I could focus on money

I would be happy?

I figured today

would be the day I left here

very well could be.

I thought of machines

to calm my anxiety

just doing their jobs.

How sad is that though?

A large source of depression

keeps heartbeats steady.

Two pages left now.

Will I quit will I quit will

I quit will I quit

I need a month off

alone and in the darkness

or on some beach, drunk.

Art

Thinking of a book.

A memoir or maybe lies.

You know, like the rest.

I am happiest

when for a moment I think

"Hey, that's not so bad."

A song, a story.

Whatever comes out of me.

Just for a moment

Because soon I see

the flaws and imperfections

and wish I was dead.

The motherfucker.

Art. What an awful life led.

Hope glimpsed but dead fast.

But there is no choice.

It's a sexuality.

It's a death sentence.

An abusive spouse.

And yet here I am, writing

haiku and dreaming.

Planning my next move

the colors I think I'll use

cardboard or canvas.

Poetry and prose.

At worst I'll find something new

and it will be trash.

And that's how it goes.

Pretending I understand

the motherfucker.

Find the purest form

of the thought to let out

make every word count.

But that's just writing.

Well, good writing, anyway.

The world just forgot.

There was always trash,

but exposure limited

and mostly cream rose.

Goddamn internet

ruined everything we know.

Well, except fucking.

And now we're silent.

Seven billion screaming out

but no one listens.

The problem I see;

everyone thinks they should speak

but I disagree.

I have found it best

to keep my goddamned mouth shut

and to go unseen.

To bring attention

usually brings problems.

I've enough of those.

Says the musician.

The man screaming at the crowd.

Goddamn hypocrite.

If I could do more

with my time and restless brain

Still won't be enough

New song recently

I am so out of practice.

Worst song I've written.

Only expression

I can use now is haiku.

At least it's something.

I could sell my art

if I knew how to sell me.

Never work again.

Write and sing and paint.

I keep my bones from creaking.

I keep you awake.

Paint won't pay the bills,

or songs, or stories or thoughts

better kill myself.

These are just boxes.

Who did Rothko think he was?

But, I like that one.

Why did Sartre write

if nothing really mattered?

Missed a syllable?

On Haiku

Want to write haiku.

I think there is too much math.

Problems, the same sum.

Write five syllables.

Then write seven syllables.

And then end with five.

These are for quick thoughts,

fleeting feeling and wordplay.

I'll figure it out.

Practice my haiku.

They are never any good.

They never will be.

This one might be good

if I really think it out.

I guess I was wrong.

So, one last attempt.

Think Asa, think you dumb shit!

Oh Christ, not again.

No no no no no

I will get it right this time.

Just plan my sylla

Wait around today.

I'm on someone else's time

Write a new haiku.

Mull over the words.

Articulate the meaning.

Always fuck it up.

It is beautiful

how haiku moves thoughts around

rearrange your heart.

Looking at Myself

I'm an alien.

You know I don't belong here.

I just want to leave.

Head stuck between ends.

I've been divided so long.

Everyone loses.

Fleetwood Mac knows me,

comforts, soothes, and walks me through.

Thunder don't need rain.

I am not this type.

Money means nothing to me.

I know I am lost.

Listen to my songs.

Sunglasses on and hid.

Nothing here is real.

Some thing I did once

and thirty other times now.

I'll keep doing it.

Try to fight drinking.

Better than I used to be.

Without, I am lost.

I am in trouble.

I am so bad at being.

I wish I was you.

Want the rain to stop.

It would be so nice to walk.

To forget myself.

Song from seventh grade

reminds me of the red house.

miss horrible times.

Can't make up my mind.

Who the fuck am I to know?

Whatever is write.

Killing time. Always.

I don't know what I wait for.

Anything, I guess.

The ship is burning.

Just... too far to swim to land.

The flames are pretty.

Been eating like shit,

drink more than you think I should.

Less than I used to.

Goddamn itching eye.

Forgot my allergy meds.

I am an adult.

Landline excitement.

Getting our new number.

I was a child.

Where do they come from?

The thoughts, plans, ideas, and dreams?

My brain is broken.

Ate a whole pizza.

Body groans and twists and dies.

Was pretty good though.

A stretch of bad luck.

Expensive bad luck, that is.

Remember old me?

Not sure how to think

or focus. Or operate.

Or live. Just pretend.

Hey, you're getting fat.

You should eat a lot more.

Never exercise.

Should get surgery.

Shrink my stomach. Cut my brain.

Be a better man.

Don't write things down yet.

You need to calm down and breathe.

Panic for nothing.

Been a while since

and now it's twice a week.

Hope it's not a trend.

Read my old haiku.

I am so fucking stupid.

A big crybaby.

Not sure if a crest

or a weightless nausea.

I don't feel as rough.

Black metal soothes me.

The unrelenting onslaught.

Comfort in a wall.

I wish I were you.

And I suppose you'd swap too.

Then, why should I care?

Can't articulate

my anxiety chokes me

sadness is nothing.

Why am I like this?

I am so tired of me.

There's no way you aren't.

Am I an average?

Not who I someday become,

but an averaged sum?

Am I not progress?

Am I not the works I've made?

Am I not "last me"?

I suppose I am

only what you remember,

whatever that is.

I am not just good

and I am not just some drunk

only what you saw.

I have earned that fate

and I suppose we all have.

That we're forgotten.

No clouds or money,

now a summer tradition.

Seasonal reset

But, it sobered me.

Fuck AA, just get me broke.

It was my sponsor.

Though I wanted to

clean up my soul for so long.

I just never could.

Always had some cash.

Five bucks here, ten or twenty.

Expensive descent.

Now I feel better

if I don't think about it.

The things I have done.

Been getting lazy.

Fat and artless and tired.

Happy or broken.

Loose Moments

Okay, a new thought.

Something a little lighter.

Fire trucks go by.

I could doze off here.

It wouldn't be the first time.

First time sober though.

Reading Tom Wolfe now.

Tried once when I was younger.

Better to me, now.

Wish I slept heavy

like everyone else seems to.

Sleep through anything...

Would be awake now,

not nodding off in this chair.

I could use a drink.

I need to get food.

I need money to get food.

Need a fucking job.

Maybe I won cash.

Maybe I can pay my bills.

My world could exhale.

The sky with no clouds

relieves us the winter passed.

Summer always is.

Had ice cream for lunch.

Thirty-three goddamn years old.

I have learned nothing.

Holes squeak in my shoes.

My thighs wear away my pants.

I can't afford new.

Library morning

all still 'June and Everything',

the most apt title.

Stealing the wi-fi

busy morning and it's slow

getting nothing done.

I could use a nap.

maybe it's the library

that makes me tired.

An itch on my leg.

It's probably a sweat bump.

I'll leave it alone.

The rocks on the lake.

I put this view on a book.

Million years ago.

Slowly wearing down

Earth dissolves against water.

Not in my lifetime.

Keeping my distance.

I see your view, understand.

It's just so awkward.

People on the shore

and the people in their boats.

I prefer the shore.

Waiting for the sun.

Got here early for a spot.

Listen to the waves.

Pools fill and I see

miniature landscapes now.

Then drain and just rocks.

Someone smoked cigars

left plastic all around here.

Don't deserve this place.

Kiss the girl hello.

Breathe in the Friday evening.

Wake up when I choose.

Three years have passed now.

Still using this book for thoughts.

This book is my heart.

Smells like weed out here.

The neighbors next door I guess.

Comforting to know.

A car pulling in.

The roar of anxiety.

Who is coming here?

This page is halfway.

For me; I'll need a new book.

You; the end of me.

Television on.

I can hear it in the house.

Fuck television.

Hear things that aren't there.

The girl is worried for me.

I am not surprised.

I was cloud bursting

at the beach, next to the girl

my shorts still weren't dry

A dog barks near us

and children bury their friends.

Last days of summer.

Somehow more lovely

than the dream of new July

and we all exhale.

"That dog," the girl says

"in a sidecar, with goggles

and he was smiling."

Goodnight my good friend.

You are the life inside of me.

And soon, the grey sky.

And vacation ends.

Not that it hadn't fucked me.

But Christ, I hate work.

Yeah, everyone does.

The fact isn't lost on me.

I keep surviving.

Now, hate something else.

Probably the wrong outlook.

I should work on that.

Walk Saratoga.

Elizabeth is at work.

Sit on a friend's porch.

In over my head.

Not responsible enough.

I will be fired.

Doomsayer, I guess.

I can change the way it goes.

Have to change my view.

Looking at Others

Like watching people

and I like taking long walks.

These things don't hurt much.

Man at the window

a break from monotony.

He pauses and breathes.

Woman in the skirt

glances sternly at the world

can't you see she works?!

Man in a blue chair.

A break from reality.

He observes and writes.

Man with jangling keys

comes into the room and leaves

"No masturbaters."

Woman with long skirt

finished her phone call and sits.

She gets back to work.

Always see notebooks

on asshole's shelves. Black leather.

Actually blank.

A band near the park.

Singing, trumpets and trombone.

They play for the rich.

I'm a bystander.

A casualty of wealth.

At least there's music.

The cool night settles

Perfect June. Almost absurd.

I am fucking broke.

There's reality;

with all of their debt

they can still get drunk,

get a steak and smile

and sway in the yellow lights.

I watch from the park.

Two men leave a bench.

It is a better bench so

I move to claim it.

Teenagers near by

recite all of their new words

and impress themselves.

Raindrops hit my arm

and I think I'll get going

Don't want to be home.

All day in the house.

Just me and the goddamned walls.

The rain's not so bad.

Three kids and two dogs.

Two well-off parents, of course.

Completely foreign.

Then sirens and lights.

Three cop cars speed into town.

Another slow night.

Steal hotel wi-fi.

Can't afford to pay my bills.

Should steal hotel cash.

"Isn't it lovely?"

they say, holding hands, walking.

"Nice to be alive."

Insensitive fucks.

And no, it goddamn isn't.

Give me your wallet.

The fantasy plays

but no one carries cash now.

It's fucking pointless.

I have to stop this.

Crashing like a burning plane.

It isn't okay.

I've ruined enough

with my nihilist bullshit

but I can't fake it.

So what do I do?

How do you change a worldview

and just be normal?

Happy? Productive?

How do I convince myself

that I can do well?

Maybe a lost cause.

Or, is that the lie again?

God fucking damnit.

ABOUT THE AUTHOR

Asa Morris lives and writes, paints and sings.

CPSIA information can be obtained
at www.ICGtesting.com
Printed in the USA
BVHW030224030421
604115BV00007B/340